SH*T GIRLS SAY

SH*T
GIRLS
SAY

KYLE HUMPHREY and GRAYDON SHEPPARD

SH*T GIRLS SAY
ISBN-13: 978-0-373-89275-4
© 2012 by Kyle Humphrey and Graydon Sheppard

Library of Congress Cataloging-in-Publication Data available

www.Harlequin.com
Printed in U.S.A.

We dedicate this book to our mothers, sisters, grandmothers, aunts, and nieces.

FRIENDS & FASHION

FROM STRANGER TO EX

That's so romantic.

BODY

ISSUES

CAN I STEAL ONE OF

YOUR FRIES?

ALL THAT

SMALL TALK AT THE PARTY

you're such a good gift-giver.

WHAT'S YOUR
DOG'S NAME?

I'm Really Good With Faces.

Is that a mojito?

I'll have
a glass of
prosecco.

EMOTIONS & INSECURITIES

*I wish I had
time to
meditate.*

Photographer
Daniel Ehrenworth
www.dephoto.org

Photographer's Assistants
Joseph Devitt Tremblay
Matthew Tammaro
John Packman

Makeup & Hair
Robert Weir

Makeup Assistants
Meaghan Bell Gregory
Kelley Cloney

Wardrobe
Corrina Allen

Art Direction, Prop Styling & Graphic Design
Kyle Humphrey
Graydon Sheppard

Kyle would like to thank:

Madison, Mom, Dad, Gummy, Gumpy,
Grandma Marge and Grandpa Helge

Graydon would like to thank:

Gramma, Mom, Dad, John, Andrew and Cindy,
Kristen and Robert, Laura and Scott,
Maeve, Lila, Will and Cole

We would like to thank:

Deb Brody,
Simon Green, Emma Thaler, and the CAA team,
Shara Alexander, Jessica Rosenberg, Maria Ribas,
Sandra Valentine, Natasa Hatsios, Gigi Lau, Margie Miller,
Amy Jones, Debbie Soares, Nicki Kommit, Larissa Walker,
Arina Kharlamova, Reka Rubin, Christine Tsai,
Donna Hayes, Loriana Sacilotto, Craig Swinwood,
Brent Lewis, Alex Osuszek, and the Harlequin team,
Michael Lasker, Brent Lilley, Justin Letter,
Ryan Pastorek, Gregg Gellman,
Kirsten Nichols, Pamela Hamilton,
Sioban Quigley, Beaux Lewis-Quigley,
Margot Arakelian, Charlotte Glynn,
Christian Buer, David Chang, Ann Cockfield,
Juliette Lewis, Stacy London, Abby Elliott,
Ali Adler, Michael Ian Black, Jiffy Wild

About the Authors

Kyle Humphrey is a graphic designer, visual artist, and writer.

Graydon Sheppard is a writer, director, and the star of *Shit Girls Say*.

Kyle and Graydon are the co-creators of *Shit Girls Say*, which started as a Twitter account in 2011 and evolved into a viral YouTube sensation later that year. The videos have garnered over 30 million views.

www.kyledavidlarsenhumphrey.com
www.graydonsheppard.com

www.ShitGirlsSay.com